BRODY THE LION

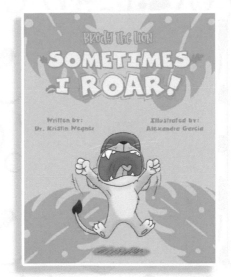

Sometimes I ROAR!

is the first book in the Brody the Lion Series. Celebrating autism while providing parents, teachers, and therapists ways to help children cope with big emotions. Sometimes I Roar depicts an autistic lion cub enjoying his birthday party. We see Brody happily flapping his paws and jumping on his toes but when his friends are late, the present is not what he expects and guests sing too loudly, Brody melts down. As he roars, Brody's parents do their best to calm their little cub using mindfulness and co-regulation strategies.

I Can Do It, Yes I Can!

Is the second book in the Brody the Lion Series. In this Book, Brody uses the positive affirmation chant 'I Can Do It, Yes I Can!' to overcome his anxieties and self-doubt. We follow Brody to ABC School and meet his teachers Dr. Roo (Kristin Kangaroo) and Mrs. G (Kimberly Giraffe). We are also introduced to Brody's Buddies who are characters inspired by children of all abilities who follow Brody the Lion. With the help of his parents, teachers and buddies Brody is the best cub that he can be.

The Shopping Flip

is Brody's third book, our favorite autistic lion cub heads to the grocery store. Despite having planned and practiced, Brody struggles with big emotions when he is faced with one unexpected event after another. From a claw game that delivers no prize to a turned over shopping cart, Brody succeeds with the help of his family and friends.
Brody's new illustrator, Fay Stayer, highlights Brody's big emotions and brings Brody's Buddies to life with captivating illustrations.

Join me on Instagram: @Brody.the.Lion or www.Brodythelion.com

This book is dedicated to every child and family
embracing the joys and facing the challenges of autism.
May Brody help you along the journey.

Characters in Brody the Lion Books
are inspired by real children. Permission has been granted
for the use of names and all information. For more information
about Brody's Buddies visit Brody's webpage.
www.BrodyTheLion.com

A special thanks to Brody's Instagram family and all who support
@Brody.the.Lion 🐾

Brody The Lion was created by
Kristin Wegner, PhD/LP
Edited by Kimberly Sattler, MS/BCBA
Published by Autism and Behavior Center, Altoona, WI.
2022 All rights reserved.
Art created digitally by Fay Stayer

rody The Lion
Meets the Doc

Written by: Dr. Kristin Wegner

Illustrated by: Fay Stayer

After Brody's birthday, the same time every year,
there was always one thing, Brody had to fear.

Brody saw the doctor, the one in the white coat,
The doctor with the stethoscope who gives you great big pokes.

Brody likes some doctors, the ones like Dr. Roo.
Dr Roo is fun, Mrs. G is too.

But even just the thought of walking through Doc's door made Brody worry and really want to ROAR.

It's OK Brody. This year will be new.
We will go and practice with G and Dr. Roo

Dr. Roo had turned the playroom into a doctor's room.
Ivy, George and Jaley were ready for a turn.

A B C D E F G H I J K

Ivy was first to go, she wasn't scared a bit.
Roo and G cheered her on, which helped her stay and sit.

Jaley was the next to go. She sat as still as could be.
Dr. Roo was proud. So was Mrs. G.

Brody's turn was next. Brody was still scared.

Brody held George's hand.
His friend was always there.

They practiced more at home, with lots of practice blows until he could say. Mom I'm good to go.

Brody filled his backpack with toys and dinosaurs
Lots of toys to play with, so Brody wouldn't roar.

At the Doc's, they had to wait, wait with all the rest.
This was the part that Brody liked best.

The room had a tank filled with lots of fish.
Getting a pet was something Brody wished.

Brody just wanted to give the fish a pet,

Brody didn't know the fish would be so wet.

Brody saw the fish flopping on the floor.

He was very worried
but Brody didn't roar.

Mama said Brody, we can all help you.
Brody took a breath and counted out to 2.

Brody started playing with the trains and the toys.
Mama didn't notice until she heard the noise.

Bear was playing with a train.
Brody thought it was his own.

Brody tried to take it
to bring the train back home

Brody started running
holding on to the train.

Brody didn't hear
when Doc called his name.

Brody kept on running until he felt a bump.
He crashed into the doctor with a mighty thump.

The doctor was just waiting, waiting patiently.

Brody took Mama's hand and headed through the door, as they did they chanted so Brody wouldn't roar.

I can do it, yes I can. I can do it, Brody can!

The next thing on the plan was the great big scale.
Brody said "I got this" and didn't even wail.

In the room and on the bed, Brody was a champ.

He did what he practiced and got a dino stamp.

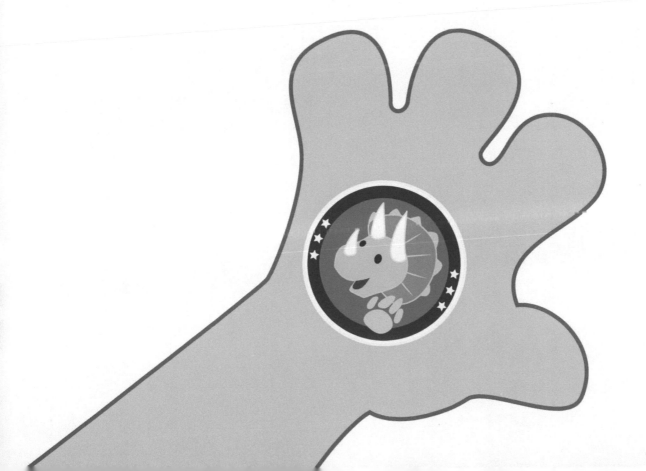

Then the time had come, for the great big shot,
Brody was still scared and squeezed Mom's hand a lot.

Brody closed his eyes, as the Doctor gave the shot.
Brody didn't roar, though it hurt a lot.

Helpful Tips

Doctor, Dentist, and Therapy appointments can be difficult for all children but for some children, these appointments lead to meltdowns. New places, unfamiliar routines, busy parking lots, crowded waiting rooms, florescent lighting, loud noises, unfamiliar smells, physical touch, invasive procedures, complex language, and difficult social situations can all be potential triggers. Here are some ways you can help:

Advocate

- Communicate with the doctor/team about your child's needs.

- Ask for what your child needs. Medical Professionals are experts in their field, but they are NOT experts when it comes to your child or Neurodiversity.

- Don't take "No" or "We don't do that here" for an answer. You know your child best. It is your right and your responsibility to advocate for your child.

- Visit the office before the appointment. Take photographs you can use for practice or to create a social story.

- Call ahead to find out exactly what will happen during your child's appointment. Ask for the first appointment in the morning or immediately after lunch.

- Set up play routines to practice what will happen during the appointment. Practice with dolls and/or stuffed animals. Have your child be the doctor and patient.

Anticipate the Unexpected

- Pack for the unexpected, include extra clothes, favorite fidget toys, ipad/-phone chargers, extra snacks and drinks, headphones, comfort items, etc.

- Before leaving for your appointment, call to see if they are running on time.

- Ask for a call or text when the Doctor/Dentist is ready to see you, so you don't have wait in waiting room.

DO

- Insist on having visits that are positive. Start by just going for a visit. If your doctor, dentist, or provider won't do this for you, find one who will.

- Follow visit with preferred activity like a trip to the park, favorite treat, or whatever activity your child loves.

- Break long appointments into several shorter appointments or take breaks. Take it slow.

- Insist that vaccines are administered on YOUR time schedule. The schedule may say your child needs 3-4 shots in one visit, but you can space them out. Don't just ask, insist for what you know your child needs.

- Bring a support person for yourself and/or your child.

- Bring your child's AAC (Communication Device).

- Ask questions when you don't understand.

- Be honest with your child. If the procedure will be painful, tell your child that it may hurt and practice strategies to cope with the pain.

DON'T

- Don't have discussions about your child in front of your child. Bring a support person that can take your child if a discussion is needed or plan in advance.

- Don't be pressured into making decisions that may not fit for your child or family.

- Don't lie to your child or minimize if they must endure a painful procedure. Telling your child "It won't hurt". This will only undermine trust.

- Don't be embarrassed by your child's behavior.

- Don't hold your child down or force a medical procedure.

Brody'S

JALEY

MARLEE

BRODY

KENNEDY

RONIN

Buddies

IVY

BARKLEY

BRODY

GENEVIEVE

GEORGE

CPSIA information can be obtained
at www.ICGtesting.com
Printed in the USA
LVHW071000211022
731075LV00041B/433